E P

RESILIENCE
LEVELLING UP HUMAN POTENTIAL

I C

Instagram   Facebook   sallydominguez.com

ISBN: 978-0-578-84033-8

Cover design by Olivia Dominguez
Space graphic by Jemima Dominguez
Layout & Coordination by Daniel Reider
Quadrant diagram by Arin Fishkin

Printed in the United States of America
First printing 2021

Adventurous Thinking Group.
Corte Madera, California, USA.

www.EPICresilience.com

Table of Contents

Introduction

If my mind can conceive it, if my heart can believe it, then I can achieve it"

- Muhammad Ali

Creative thinking has nothing to do with artistry.
Creative thinking is about mental growth.

WHY START A BOOK ON RESILIENCE with creative thinking? Because a growth mindset and the ability to not just survive but also thrive in unpredictable change relies on creative thinking. Creative is a word loaded with implications of artistic expression, sketching prowess and other craft and manual-skill-related talents. Because of its close association with art, many people shut off when they hear "creative thinking." They don't realize that every human brain has the ability to think creatively and every person, given the right tools, is able to vastly improve their ability to imagine ideas and make the unexpected connections that hallmark innovation and growth. Traditional rational thinkers need to understand the importance of creative thinking and the growth mindset that it represents. In an era where rapid change renders much of our knowledge outdated or irrelevant, creative thinking needs to become our default tool for strategy and problem-solving. Think creatively, then use knowledge and experience to galvanize that thought into action.

Old school resilience was about toughing it out. We were simply required to survive a disturbing event basically intact. Once the event was over the assumption was that the survivors could then revert to "normal" life.

We ask for more of resilience in 2020 and beyond as we navigate an era where unpredictable change has become the norm. Every vertical of business and society is being disrupted. We are exposed to a relentless wave of disturbing events. As psychologist Abraham Maslow says, "you will either step forward into growth, or backward into safety." In this era, backward into safety means falling into the backwash of a massive change wave. There is no safe place to wait it out.

EPIC Resilience means riding that wave with confidence, not being left in its wake. We need to be physically and mentally strong just to survive the exhaustion of being constantly alert, but we also need to get in front of that wave with growth and vision. That means developing the habit of creative thinking and making that thinking muscle as strong and used as our expertise muscle is. There is no one event to survive in 2020 and beyond: resilience today means weathering and flourishing in uncertainty. Personally, and as a community. Hence EPIC Resilience, the balance of Emotional, Physical, Intellectual and Creative habits that starts with individual self-awareness and optimization, but applies equally to families, communities and business culture. Developing, honing and constantly fine-tuning our Emotional, Physical, Intellectual and Creative quadrants ensures that we face this new era with optimism and confidence.

In 2012 I was invited to drive with my best mate across Morocco in the Rallye des Gazelles. We would be the first Australians to drive this 9-day race and it presented some unique challenges: electronics were banned, we were to navigate the highest dunes and mountains in the country, and some of the most extreme terrain, with compasses and old topographic maps and - the whole thing was in French. The other teams spent a month prepping in Morocco but the Aussies were an afterthought so we had less than two weeks notice and no training in map and compass navigation or extreme sand driving. Clearly Volkswagen had great faith in Sammy and I....

Long story short: the reason European camera teams follow this all-female extreme race is for the emotional breakdowns that pepper the field. Team after team succumbs to the stress of intense heat, endless sand dunes, dodgy belly, fatigue alternating with Red Bull-fueled manic bursts and the monotony of flat tires, digging out in the dunes and French army rations. This was possibly the hardest challenge I have undertaken - but I loved it! I reveled in the open desert, I dug with gusto when we hit camel grass, MacGyver'd our way out of multiple dramas and led a car-top disco dance (we were the only car using music while racing) when we finally traversed the X-Route over the Erg Chebi dunes. Why, I wondered, was I feeling so free when the women around me were dropping like flies? Everyone was physically fit and prepared. Everyone had essentially the same tools and the same spirit of adventure. What differed some from others, I realized, was mental stamina and creative thinking. Confronted continuously for nine days with unexpected hazards some racers threw their hands in the air and gave up. They didn't KNOW the answers to the challenges they faced, and they didn't have the tools to wonder and problem-solve in the unknown. Others, like us, stopped, figured out a quick fix, assisted if we could and then took off again, whooping into the unknown.

When you are OK with not knowing, and when you are constantly curious, you free yourself to learn on the fly and to imagine - and enact - new ways of solving problems. This is creative thinking: the ability to wonder combined with the confidence to try your own ideas out.

In the Rallye knowledge and certainty took a back seat to adventure and chaos, forcing racers to tap into their less-used mental resources. It helped me realize that my inventive mind, my imagination and my curiosity equip me to relish uncertainty as an adventure to be had. As the motto of the Rallye des Gazelles notes, *It is in the loss of landmarks that the Gazelles find their true values.* EPIC Resilience is about assessing your landscape and shedding the superfluous limits that are not part of your essential value set so that your values and boundaries are clear to you and to everybody else. EPIC is about the freedom and confidence to think and do on the fly. This is how we will all thrive in a world that will continue to change too fast for knowledge to keep up.

Before I wrote this book I traveled the world driving concept cars in exotic locations and teaching Adventurous Thinking, an innovation strategy I designed based on the theory of multiple intelligences (more on that later). Before that I judged invention and innovation on Australian television. In Australia I had invented two products, a high chair and a rainwater tank, that redefined their respective markets by combining "high design" with functionality. First, I was told that the baby furniture market would never want a "designer" product. That was in 2003. My product, NEST high chair, won several design awards, featured in numerous editorials, redefined the baby furniture market and is now held in at least two museums. Two years later exploring another concept I was told that it was impossible to store water vertically in a flat-walled plastic tank. With no expertise in plastics manufacturing I pushed to realize my design and pioneered a new structural design for rotomolded tanks that has become the norm in a new category called "slim-walled" tanks. My Rainwater HOG tank has won more than five international awards to date. In both instances I was reminded by experts in each category that I was an architect, not a product designer. That I had no experience with plastics. That I was bound to fail.

Clearly being told by experts that something won't work has never resonated with me. As I began to work more with other innovators, first in television and then during my teaching at Stanford University and my work at Singularity University, I realized that this healthy disregard for the opinions of others is the common trait of pioneers and innovators. This trait is better known today as "embracing failure" and it means that while we respect knowledge we are also well aware that knowledge is limited by what we know in the present, and that our future is determined by our imagination and our curiosity to know more. Proceeding, therefore, knowing that the experts have put the kibosh on our idea, means we understand it is high risk but we still think it's worth trying.

The other common trait I observed in consistently innovative people is their habit of mentally walking around an issue or design curiously prodding it from many directions. When the Powerhouse Museum asked me to explain my design process to busloads of Design Technology teachers and their students I was stumped, because my thinking is so swirly. Then I realized: this is how all those other innovators think too! I dug into Professor Howard Gardner's book, *Frames of Mind: The Theory of Multiple Intelligences,* and all became clear. Rational thinking - knowledge-based thinking - is just one of up to eleven ways of assessing and problem solving. Inspired by the potential of multiple intelligences to explain this swirl approach to ideation and problem-solving, I constructed five Lenses designed to throw a person's brain out of the comfort zone of expertise and into the bearable discomfort of not knowing. Possibility thinking. These Five Lenses - Negative Space, Sideways, Backwards, ReThinking and Parkour - are the basis of my Adventurous Thinking strategy which I teach at Stanford, Singularity and to various organizations around the world. As Gartner observes, "it's not how smart you are that matters, what really counts is how you are smart." A reliance on linear thinking, based on knowledge and rationale, means you are ill-equipped to grapple with sudden change and a plethora of variables. A confidence in your ability to work in the realm of possibility is the hallmark of visionary thinking.

What do these characteristics mean in terms of resilience? Obviously there is tenacity and a refusal to give up, but more than that is the habit of thinking beyond what we know, and delving into the realm of what could be. This terrific analogy from MIT Professor George Westerman nails old school "survive" resilience versus new era EPIC "thrive" resilience. Westerman refers to digital transformation, but his analogy pertains to all thinking that is incremental and knowledge-based rather than imagination-based. Westerman says; "When digital transformation is done right it's like a caterpillar turning into a butterfly. But when done wrong all you have is a really fast caterpillar." As we experience societal norms and entire business verticals disrupting, even the fastest caterpillar will be left behind. Making small improvements, relying on expertise and status quo thinking, waiting for things to return to "normal", and being risk-averse in the face of change will never allow you to control your circumstance. Treading water only keeps you alive while you wait for someone else to rescue you. To thrive in chaos and uncertainty we need big, powerful, capable, disruptive thinking. EPIC Resilience delivers the strength and transformative thinking to lead the change that is inevitable.

I.
Finding Opportunity in Chaos

RESILIENCE IS MUCH MORE THAN GRIT. Grit helps you weather the storm but once you have survived you need to thrive: to actively harness the energy of change and propel yourself to new horizons and new opportunities. Hence EPIC. EPIC represents the balance of your Emotional, Physical, Intellectual, and Creative aspects of self. EPIC is a strategy that connects your physical and mental potential with Adventurous Thinking, holistically addressing our mental and physical strength along with your ability and confidence to spot an opportunity, seize it and innovate. EPIC Resilience considers these four essential aspects of you as interconnected Quadrants, and together they dictate your robust personal Resilience. This book aims to provoke a self-awareness of the EPIC Quadrants that make up our character and affect our own ability to spring forward, harness change, and provide the tools to maintain that edge while practicing optimism and constant innovation. Futurist and inventor Buckminster Fuller declared, "If you want to teach people a new way of thinking, don't bother trying to teach them. Instead, give them a tool, the use of which will lead to new ways of thinking." EPIC Resilience is the tool that you need to survive, navigate and flourish in change as well as in normal daily life. By improving your awareness of self, EPIC will tune up your overall health and wellbeing while increasing your confidence and innovative potential.

Why does so much of our education and day-to-day interaction value rational thinking and knowledge over imagination and adaptability?

It's almost as if our thinking values haven't changed since the Industrial Revolution and the advent of factory thinking...oh, wait... it hasn't.

We should first be thinking big - in the realm of possibility, imagination and moonshot - then using our knowledge to help realize that vision.

EPIC Resilience is about preparing ourselves for the inevitable uncertainty and constant change that comes with this new era of digitization, exponential information sharing, technological challenge and social upheaval. This is an era where our knowledge cannot keep up with the speed of change - which means we need to develop a new kind of thinking that is not the knowledge-based expertise we have come to rely on. Imagination, in the form of creative confidence and the ability to ask questions, will define this new era.

This new age is known as the Fourth Revolution, a cataclysm marked by the transcendence of technology. Many futurists see this era culminating with the "Singularity" where humans and machines merge into a cyborg-type existence. In this future most white collar jobs and much of the manual

"Imagination is more important than knowledge. For knowledge is limited, whereas imagination embraces the entire world, stimulating progress, giving birth to evolution"

- Albert Einstein

labor - ultimately even some creative thinking - currently handled by humans will be carried out by machines. Humans, the forecasters say, will be freed from their old-school nine-to-five grind to think creatively with an abundance of leisure time. Such a future bears no relationship to society's current predilection for linear, knowledge-based reasoning.

This era of upheaval, as momentous and transformational for humankind and the planet as the Industrial Revolution before it, creates an unrelenting wave of change that will either lift us up, or dump us under. But as machine learning and refinement accelerates exponentially, humans are generally less curious and less proactive than in previous eras. Our reliance on the internet to provide answers has dulled our ability to ask hard questions. Our self-awareness focuses on social worth and the opinions of others rather than the abilities we hold within ourselves. Witness the widespread panic when cities lose power and internet access for even short amounts of time. People are as thrown by the lack of ready online access as they are by the lack of electricity itself. People are accustomed to a level of white noise and online chatter that may sooth in its distraction but seldom helps us take stock, assess the situation and make confident decisions on our own. **WE CAN DO BETTER.**

Sebastian Junger is a journalist and filmmaker who observes humans operating in extreme conditions. In his book, *Tribe*, Junger notes, "Humans don't mind hardship, in fact they thrive on it; what they mind is not feeling necessary." Facing change makes many people feel insignificant and unnecessary. Why? Because most of us are rarely asked to think or do anything outside our daily comfort zone. Simply put, people are not taught the value of self awareness, the reward of physical and mental challenge or the tools to think outside expertise and knowledge. Most people don't understand that the limits they see around their lives and their abilities are self-imposed.

The threat of change feels overwhelming because people are unaware that the human brain and the human body - your brain, your body - is capable of so much more than we give it credit for. The current upheavals in every area of society have many people fearing the future because society generally values knowledge and expertise over imaginative thinking. Our emphasis on specialization and rational learning leaves people unpracticed in thinking from first principles and unaccustomed to creative problem solving as a serious strategy for survival and growth. Understand that this fear and these limits are negotiable. EPIC establishes a level of self awareness to ensure your mental and physical stability and develops a flexible mindset based on curiosity, possibility and imagination. EPIC draws upon motivational psychology, Adventurous Thinking, the theory of multiple intelligences and ancient Stoic philosophy to level up humans with a proactive, optimistic and creatively confident self awareness that enables us to realize and celebrate the full potential of the human brain and the human

> *"It is not the strongest of the species that survives, nor the most intelligent, but the one most responsive to change"*
>
> - Charles Darwin

body. Your brain. Your body. At any age. In any circumstance.

Resilience doesn't require adversity to be an effective strategy: strength and a growth mindset deliver everyday benefits. However, the ability to lead with optimism in times of uncertainty is a huge advantage. You never know when your world will be bumped off its axle. EPIC Resilience fortifies your body and mind and optimizes your skill set to help you find opportunity in chaos and joy in the everyday, using the Quadrants to check in and balance, and the Ring of Intent to constantly grow and improve our individual resilience holistically.

First, the EPIC strategy helps you understand what the Quadrants are and how they affect your overall resilience. The Emotional and Physical Quadrants are concerned with fulfilling our basic human needs for a strong and resilient foundation. Establishing constant human Connection is also part of this self-balance to improve Competency and Authenticity. The Intellectual and Creative Quadrants push personal development past our basic need for stability and move towards self actualization by developing our growth mindset and realizing our full potential for innovative thinking.

"Until you make the unconscious conscious, it will direct your life and you will call it fate"

- CG Jung

Next we examine what your Quadrants currently look like in terms of strengths and weaknesses. The Balance chapter uses a quiz and the Quadrant diagram to set your Line in the Sand and proposes an Action Checklist to help you level up the weaker areas to match your strengths. Balancing your Quadrants should also activate your creative confidence as you begin to understand yourself better and realize your full potential.

Finally EPIC encourages you to share that optimism and confidence with others, focusing on Connection and Purpose. This is a strategy that scales from individual to organizational level for productive resilience and an inclusive, creative culture.

The essence of the EPIC strategy is simple: to have sustainable impact in your relationships, in your family, in your workplace and your communities you need to be in peak shape emotionally, physically, intellectually and creatively. This is akin to the first rule of flying: put your own oxygen mask on first so that you can then effectively assist others.

Mario Quintana puts it more poetically: "Don't waste your time chasing butterflies. Mend your garden and the butterflies will come."

"What you do makes a difference, and you have to decide what kind of difference you want to make"

- Jane Goodall

II.
Understanding the Quadrants

EPIC BALANCES HEALTHY SELF-AWARENESS AND PHYSICAL toughness with intellectual and creative confidence. Once balanced, EPIC Resilience inspires optimism and effective outreach. EPIC strives to realize all the potential you have to offer, for the betterment of yourself and the people around you. EPIC considers four inter-dependent areas of your body and your character that are essential to resilience and identifies them as: Emotional, Physical, Intellectual and Creative. These are referred to as your Quadrants.

Surviving: Emotional Resilience

Values and Boundaries

Emotional stability is the backbone of resilience and addressing your Emotional Quadrant starts with self examination. Resiliency is the ability to function effectively and independently of others. Functioning autonomously requires self-awareness and that starts with valuing yourself. Once you understand your own value you will set and maintain boundaries that make your value clear to others. Your boundaries, based as they are on your values, stay essentially the same. From that base you will continually re-invigorate and extend your outreach, building connections that become part of your growth.

Clear boundaries demonstrate what you value and what you will and will not accept in your life. Boundaries ensure you make important decisions about your values ahead of time, and strong boundaries mean you have one less level of decision-making on the fly. This sense of self is the bedrock of resilience. Think of your boundaries as the buttresses that keep you upright and secure. Some people maintain solid boundaries without really thinking about it. Others scoff at the concept of "boundaries" which usually means those people feel threatened. Ask yourself why. It is never too late to consciously map out your boundaries and make them known to others. You will immediately feel the security and peace of mind that this firm setting of personal values delivers.

Here is an example from my own values and boundary work. I hugely value trust, transparency and honesty. My boundary statement is thus, "I will not tolerate a pattern of lying. If I discover that someone I am interacting with is engaged in a pattern of deceptive behavior I will make it clear that they are not welcome on my property or in my circle while that behavior persists."

Clearly communicating your values along with your boundaries ensures that anyone interacting with you hears the what and the why. It gives other people every opportunity to understand you and your

> " 'NO' is a complete sentence"
>
> - Annie Lamott

actions better. It lays out the behavior you consider unacceptable, and the consequences for that behavior in terms of a relationship with you. Locking the values and the statement together make your motivations clear.

What is NOT a boundary statement? A friend recently shared this post-therapy statement from her partner which references "boundaries" but not values: "My boundary is Do not speak while I am thinking." This is not a boundary statement. It does not reflect that person's values or speak to their intent. This statement is simply a rule or request which includes the word "boundary." A Boundary is not an instruction to others or an action. It is a limit with guidelines set by you to reflect your values.

Setting Your Values

This is a 30-minute exercise to focus and hone your key values and boundaries. It is an essential step to emotional balance and stability.

Write a list of five values that are important to you. Some examples of values people might consider important are reliability, trust, transparency, fiscal prudence, respect, inclusion, creative freedom, independence, adventure, compassion. There are many more. Once you write your own list of values consider each one for at least five minutes.

Poke and prod at this concept to tease out the details that are important to you. Ask yourself questions: Why is this important to me? How does it currently play out in my life? In what situations am I receiving or not receiving this thing that I value? How often is this value challenged, provoked or ignored in a way that makes me uncomfortable? Write yourself notes or doodles as you think about each value. Scratching pen on paper helps your working memory process new thinking more effectively. Doodling while learning is also an important habit to develop for your Intellectual and Creative Quadrants. Back to the Values list.

For each individual value consider which people are disrespecting this value. Are they family? Friends? Work colleagues? Why are they disrespecting this value? Are they unaware that it is important to you? Are you communicating it clearly to the people in those various categories? Are you enforcing this value?

As an aside you might wonder, why focus on the people who disrespect? Why go to the negative? Generally we like to focus on the positive, and on people and ideas that reaffirm what we are comfortable with. This is an aspect of confirmation bias that we all have. EPIC is about pushing you out of that comfort zone and into those areas of bearable discomfort that make you tougher and stronger. Authentic self awareness and resilience requires the ability to face the negative head on and deal with it effectively. As we force ourselves to face negative aspects and people rather than pretend

"Disrespect is not a valuation of your worth but a signal of their character"

- Brendon Burchar

they don't exist, we realize how little power others really have over our well-being and progress. This realization is an essential part of EPIC growth.

Epictetus was a Greek slave and philosopher renowned for the power of his Stoic ethics. One of his most significant observations is this: "When someone is properly grounded in life, they shouldn't have to look outside themselves for approval."

"I've been popular and unpopular successful and unsuccessful loved and loathed and I know how meaningless it all is. Therefore I feel free to take whatever risks I want"

- Madonna

If this Values exercise is frustrating you with its digging and questioning of your personal limits, ask yourself why. Are you a pleaser avoiding upset? Are you a skeptic who finds the very concept of boundaries a bit "woo-woo"? These are all important insights into yourself. Tackling your personal values and developing a disciplined self awareness is an important part of personal resilience. It can be uncomfortable, but it is absolutely worth the effort. Once you have asked the hard questions around each value, and established that these are indeed the values that define you, consider how you need to amplify each of these values in order to remind yourself of them, and to communicate your strong boundaries to other people.

Write a strong boundary statement for each of your five values, defining what is and isn't acceptable to you around this value. I shared one of my Boundary statements around trust and truth in the introduction to this Chapter. Construct each statement to include the values it enforces, the behaviors you consider unacceptable and the consequences for those behaviors. This is an important step towards greater self awareness.

Here is that example again, with a break down. "I will not tolerate a pattern of lying." This identifies truthfulness and transparency as one of my core values, and clearly states that a pattern of deceit falls outside my accepted limits. "If I discover that someone I am interacting with is engaged in a pattern of deceptive behavior I will make it clear that they are not welcome on my property or in my circle while that behavior persists." This statement lays out the consequences of the unacceptable behavior but also leaves space for a person to change that unacceptable behavior and be included. I refer myself to this statement when my emotions are running high to help with decision making and to generally de-stress. Knowing your value limits is empowering.

Use questions to tease out what you are really looking for and what you are truly representing. Questions are an essential part of a growth mindset. It can also be helpful to search for quotes around this value that resonate with you. Sometimes other people's words can suggest exactly what you are thinking. The quotes scattered throughout this book are thoughts that resonate with me and help me stay inspired and purposeful. Some of them are pinned in my office and I use them to check in on myself, others feature in my keynotes on innovation and Adventurous Thinking. Consider creating a visual reminder for your personal space using quotes and images to represent the boundaries you are maintaining and the aspirations you have.

Sharing these Value and Boundary creations and inspirations with friends, family and work colleagues, online or in person, is another way to ensure your values are clearly understood and respected. Sharing this kind of thinking starts interesting - albeit sometimes difficult - conversations, and inspires others to think harder about their own values and boundaries. Those conversations and that inspiration leads us to the other component of your Emotional Quadrant: Connection.

Be aware of the relationships that are comfortable, the relationships that are inspiring, and those that have simply aged out. Change is part of growth.

Connection

Connecting with people every day is important to maintaining your emotional equilibrium. Humans are literally wired to connect. We have empathy, which is basically the ability to feel and understand other people's emotions, and we have interbrain synchrony, a less-understood phenomenon where teams of co-operating humans reach a "flow" state with a unique cognitive rhythm. So developing the habit of connection is simply reinforcing a tendency and an inclination that we were all designed for.

In addition to creating an emotional support network, reaching out to people every day builds a connection muscle that makes you more able to lead if you choose. Connection with others and being available to listen is a core tenet of Emotional Resilience. It is important, however, that you determine your boundaries first. **These connections are about growth. They are not about validation.**

Your Emotional Quadrant considers two aspects of human connection:

1. Your ability to effectively communicate your boundaries to others, and to eliminate from your circle and disconnect from those people who do not respect your boundaries.

2. Your ability to meaningfully connect with a diverse range of people and to develop continuous connection into a daily habit.

The ability to filter people who do not meet your value criteria is empowering and very valuable. If you find a person constantly breaching your values, limit the energy you expend trying to control or convince them. Instead practice loving detachment, which means removing emotion from the interaction and trying as much as possible to avoid arguing, giving advice or otherwise investing in their actions. When renowned poet Rumi observed that "Life is a balance between holding and letting go" he was referring to the power of release. Hanging on - whether its physical or emotional - can drain you and exhaust you. When you finally release yourself, your energy will immediately start to replenish. Letting go of a depleting

> *"If you look at the people in your circle and you don't get inspired then you don't have a circle. You have a cage."*
>
> - Nipsea Hustle

relationship may be one of the most difficult things you do but self preservation is essential to resilience. Filtering people is hard but it makes you stronger.

As we live our lives through various stages - school, the workplace - we are thrown together with people with whom we learn to co-exist. Learning to co-exist with disparate personalities is an ability we learn from early school days and this ability means you have emotional intelligence. Being able to handle without emotional effect people who you might not necessarily choose to connect with outside an organization is an important part of resilience made easier and more effective by your strong boundaries.

But while tolerating relationships as part of a larger picture is very much a part of work and life it is also perfectly valid to grow out of friendships, or to respect the memory of a relationship but leave it behind. Being able to take a "birds eye" view of a situation and impartially consider the elements and repercussions of a situation or relationship is a valuable aspect of resilience worth developing. As you become secure with your beliefs and boundaries you are able to better see the true colors of others. Choose who you spend time with. You now have EPIC vision!

Forming the Habit of Connection

Once you have determined that your boundaries are strong and clear, examine whether you have the habit of daily connection. Research has found that the one habit more effective than any other in bolstering happiness and self-worth in humans is actively, without ulterior motive, reaching out to 3 people every day. This habit is proven to have more effect than gratitude journals and more effect than vision boards.

This is not to downplay gratitude, with its strong connection to self-esteem, mental health and optimism. Gratitude is one of your personal tools for self awareness and growth, and gratitude reduces a multitude of toxic emotions including envy, resentment and regret. However, connection ultimately has greater impact because it simultaneously benefits you and other people and such impact is an essential part of resilience and leadership. Connection shares your confidence and optimism with others, rippling your positive energy outwards and increasing your impact in the world.

So consider what connection means to you. Is "staying in touch" part of your daily routine or is it something that does not come naturally to you? Is your current outreach consistent or do you need to build that habit? Some days it can be hard to put in the effort of outreach. Ask yourself why that might be. Are you unhappy with your current status and not wanting to share it? Not feeling "up to conversation"? Take the time to gain insights around how connection currently looks for you and why that may be. Understanding your hesitation is the key to overcoming it.

> *"Loving yourself and others unconditionally is a balance between protecting yourself and giving to others"*
>
> - yung pueblo

A Tool for Prompting Connection

A time management friend gave me a great tool for maintaining a pipeline of business connections. This same tool will help you build and strengthen the habit of connection until you no longer need an aid. You might scoff at the artifice of a "tool for connection" but making this a daily habit can be harder than you think, especially on off days, and this tool simply helps you reach out every day without overthinking it.

Using Excel or some other spreadsheet tool, make a list on the vertical of everybody you can think of: family, friends, friends of friends, old work colleagues, people you admire and wish you knew better. Think big: you may be surprised how open to connection the people you hugely admire can be. The horizontal is a record of what date you made contact, any notes you want to make on the content of the conversation, and then a third and fourth column for future outreach.

The idea is that you make contact and have a chat or leave a message. Remember - this is not about networking. It is not about a blunt career ask. This is about genuine interest, a shared experience or idea or a question. Be authentic. Let people know how you are feeling, what you are thinking and why you are reaching out. It can be as simple as, "I am practicing a strategy of EPIC Resilience and trying to improve my ability to connect with interesting people. I sincerely admire the work you created/the research you spearheaded/your teaching…." Whatever it is you feel. Then you need to add something that the person can respond to. I am a big fan of recommended reading or viewing. "Could you please recommend a book/TV series

/artwork that you find inspiring?" perhaps. Or "What do you think of (insert interesting idea or thought piece)?" The Intellectual and Creative Quadrants talk more about idea-sharing. Use what you learn to create a note that inspires a response.

Record the date and content. Digest the response. If you don't get a response, don't take it personally. There are many reasons why someone might not receive a message, or might not respond. Depending on the response, in two to three weeks time connect again. Be sure to connect with one new person on this list every day for the first two weeks. If you are energized by this amount of outreach, try talking with two people every day. The tool takes the thinking out of the interaction: just work your way down the list, starting with the easy people and building up confidence for new connections. And yes - it is a fantastic tool for building a business contact pipeline also.

If this concept of structured outreach remains uncomfortable let's commence a change now! Remember your ultimate power is over your own mind. Any limits and hesitations you have are in your mind and only you are able to change and shape your mind. A growth mindset means we tackle our discomfort head on. So - commit yourself to a week of outreach so that you can feel the difference that proactively seeking human connection can bring. Put yourself in the shoes of the people receiving your note. How would you feel if someone contacted you and said they were interested in your ideas or work? Wouldn't that be a valuable thing to receive? At worst you will overcome a personal mental barrier. At best you will build a vibrant web of community. You have nothing to lose but your fear!

Surviving: Physical Resilience

Some of the brightest scientific and engineering minds are working deep inside NASA's Innovation Labs working to invent longer lasting, more efficient pumps for future settlement on Mars. Despite their access to the most cutting edge technologies they say that the most efficient pump by far remains the human heart. We too easily take for granted the incredible and complex living machine that is our body.

Physical resilience is about ensuring your body provides a solid foundation for your survival. You build that strength from within. The mind/body connection is the foundation of physical resilience.

Innovative trauma psychiatrist Dr Bessel van der Kolk is an expert in the way trauma manifests itself in our physical body. Describing that very direct relationship between state of mind and state of body he says, "Being frightened means that you live in a body that is always on guard. Angry people live in angry bodies....In order to change, people need to become aware of their sensations and the way that their bodies interact with the world around them. Physical self-awareness is the first step in releasing

"You have brains in your head, you have feet in your shoes, you can steer yourself any direction you choose"

- Dr Seuss

the tyranny of the past." Simply put, physical resilience is not just about what you are eating or how you are moving. Its also about what you are thinking and saying. So, in addition to optimizing the physical aspects of your being, working on your Emotional, Intellectual and Creative Quadrants will profoundly affect your level of Physical resilience.

If your Line in the Sand assessment reveals that your Physical Quadrant is relatively weak, examine what and how you eat, how you move and how much you move every day, and your sleep habits. Good nutrition mends cells and fortifies your gut and organs. Physical fitness ensures you have strength and endurance. Deep sleep, resulting from both those habits, cleanses the brain and processes memories. Improving physical resilience decreases stress reactivity, which means that in a stressful situation physically fit and healthy people are less likely to suffer stress-related disorders and inflammation. Exercise and good nutrition increases serotonin levels and decreases cortisol levels, making your body stronger and your mind stable.

In times of uncertainty, many people deprioritize physical fitness and nutritional health. Ensuring you are constantly fortified from the inside out primes you physically

"Physical fitness is not only one of the most important keys to a healthy body, it is the basis of dynamic and creative intellectual activity"

- John F. Kennedy

to deal with stress, uncertainty and quick decision-making. A strong Physical Quadrant means that you are functioning at your peak physical potential most days. Maintaining a strong Physical Quadrant means at any moment of drama or change you will hit the ground running.

What you eat

What you eat dictates your body's health. In terms of resilience that means understanding what your body needs and ensuring it can get what it requires to function efficiently. This is not about counting calories but simply awareness about the vitamins and minerals your body needs, and where you are getting those from.

Be aware of what your eating habits are and whether they match your nutritional requirements. It never hurts to stop and assess habits that have developed over years. Have you adjusted your diet and habits to suit your change in age? Have you switched from working in an office to working at home or vice versa and how has that affected your physical habits?

If you sit at a computer most of the day and you have snacks to keep you upbeat, energized and focused, have a think about how you came to choose those and whether they are actually helping. Do a quick checklist of your average intake and consider whether there is enough protein and fiber versus sugar and fat. If you are a coffee person stop and assess whether large amounts of milk or sugar are creeping into that beverage. Like every part of EPIC, change and upgrade starts with being self aware. What is it that you consume, and why have you chosen those items? What effect are you hoping they will have?

Now consider the impact that disaster or disruption could have on your ability to fuel yourself. If you had to survive with limited resources would you know how to eat effectively? Is the food you eat locally sourced or is it shipped in? If restaurants and stores closed what are your food options? Is there anything you could grow in a benchtop microgarden or an outside area that would add fresh content to the mix?

Consider how often you prepare food at home and what it is that you use. Why is it that you eat what you eat? Do you seek out sugar or salt when you are stressed? Do you like to graze or do you prefer a few large meals? Do you plan your eating in advance? Get to know yourself and understand the reasons that you have made these food decisions for yourself. Was it based on convenience? Price? Limited time? Is there a better way?

American anthropologist Margaret Mead noted that "it is easier to change a man's religion than to change his diet." Our eating patterns quickly become habits that we rarely think about. Resilience entails being aware of your tendencies and activating strategies that minimize those conditions and give you more control over them. Optimizing your Physical Quadrant sets your body up for success.

Physical optimization is a proven way to naturally combat stress and depression. For instance, multiple studies have found a correlation between a diet high in refined sugars and impaired brain function including a worsening of symptoms of mood disorders, such as depression. If you tend to be anxious or suffer bouts of depression, consider the food you eat with those tendencies in mind. You would want to minimize highly processed foods and add nuts, fresh fruit, vegetables and sources of Omega-3 fatty acids to generally feel healthier and more in control. Take the time and make the effort to understand yourself, acknowledge your tendencies, habits and areas of vulnerability and actively take control of improving what you can. This is resilience.

Eating less processed foods, more fruits and vegetables and less animal fat also creates a more healthy microbiome and decreases inflammation. The microbiome is a fascinating ecosystem inside us well worth investigating. Your microbiome is unique. Originally determined by your DNA, then your mother's microbiota, then your environmental exposures and diet, scientists are continually discovering more about the role it plays in our health and wellbeing. Commercially available kits can help you get a snapshot of what your microbiome looks like and how it might be improved to make you feel more energetic and healthy. This is yet another window into your unique physical system and how it might best operate.

A quick ditty on added sugar. The World Health Organization suggests we eat no more than 5-10 teaspoons of added sugar per day but the average American eats 17 teaspoons (the FDA suggests up to 12.5 teaspoons which reeks of industry lobbyists) and the average Australian is at 12.5 teaspoons. Why

"Take care of your body. It's the only place you have to live"

- Jim Rohn

the focus on sugar? Because a recent 15-year Harvard study showed that excess sugar is directly related to heart disease, regardless of whether the eater has an otherwise healthy diet. Thus the first step in optimizing your overall health is to try reducing your added sugar intake to the recommended maximum. If, like me, you keep a stash of chocolate for "emergencies" ask yourself why, in a moment of stress, is sugar your go-to? Perhaps there is something more remedial that you simply haven't thought of. For me it was rediscovering the comfort factor of fresh peaches and berries that helped me reduce (not end!) the intake of my beloved Belgian milk chocolate. Again, taking the time to reflect on entrenched habits can help you make the tweaks and changes that will optimize your health and strength.

How you move

Physical resilience is as much about being aware of your body's unique characteristics and abilities as it is about actual exercise. It is about physical health and physical strength. The more in tune you are with your physical state the better prepared you are to use your physicality at any moment. The only way to really get in tune with your body and understand it is to try a variety of different movements and feel how your body responds. In particular look for your physical strength. How strong are you? How strong do you feel? Do you incorporate impact and explosive strength into your daily movement?

The interesting thing about the movement component of physical fitness is that there are so many approaches to try. A short burst of jumps or squats in the middle of your day can feel fantastic - if that has never occurred to you give it a go! For those of us who embrace explosive power exercises, slow core and yoga can be an interesting extension. As our bodies get older resistance and weight exercise becomes an important part of maintaining skeletal health. Ironically, many people reduce their vigorous exercise as they age despite the science that endorses weights and energy bursts as an important way to maintain bone density and muscle strength. I began boxing when I turned 49 and hitting the heavy bag every second day has me feeling more powerful than I ever have. This parlays into having consistently higher energy along with greater confidence enforcing my boundaries. I am more productive and have better peace of mind. I also sleep more soundly. The spill-on effect of improving your physical strength is real.

> "The pain you feel today will be the strength you feel tomorrow"
>
> - Arnold Schwarzenegger

Perhaps you do not consider yourself "sporty"? Please don't check out of this Quadrant! Remember, trying an aspect of movement that you've never considered is a huge part of your mental growth and the growth mindset we address in the Intellectual Quadrant. Trying a new vigorous or strenuous movement will give you some insight into the potential you hold within your biggest muscles. As soon as you experience the burn of a few deep squats or weighted arm lifts you will quickly understand that your body is just busting for you to pay it some attention so that it can reward you with faster reflexes, clearer thinking and deeper sleep.

If you have limiting health issues get creative. If you cant use your arms you can still deep squat. If your knees are bad your arms can still lift weights in any number of different ways. This is about proactively finding physical power where you can, and that relentless searching is resilience.

Here are a few movements for anybody, regardless of a "sport" mindset, to build a better relationship with your body.

A. Squat with what you've got   If you have never lifted weights, the important thing to bear in mind is that this action is all about a solid core. That means you need to clench your gut muscles and straighten your back as you carry out this movement. Find something fairly heavy - a stable stack of books, a box of cans or maybe a stool. Stand with feet shoulder width apart holding your weight. Straighten your back, tighten the gut muscles and slowly lower into a deep squat keeping your back straight and your tummy muscles tight. Feel the weight through your leg muscles and glutes. Feel the solidity of your core muscles and understand the advantages that a strong core can bring to the rest of the body. Repeat that deep weighted squat four times and feel the potential of those big leg muscles.

B. Can your cans   Take two cans of the same weight, one in each hand. Tighten your gut muscles, stand straight and extend your arms straight out like wings, holding the cans perpendicular to the ground. Slowly "flap" your straight arms an inch up and an inch down and feel your arm muscles take on the extra weight of the cans. Feel the potential of your body and what it can do for you.

C. Shock n Awe. If your movement is usually gentle - say yoga, pilates, hiking - consider a dash of vigorous movement into your daily routine to explore other aspects of your body potential. For instance, jumping jacks or running stairs for a total five minutes. Burpees or mountain climbers are easily done anywhere - try three minutes a day. Jump out of bed and run for five minutes. A quick shock of exercise every day jumpstarts your serotonin and primes your body for unexpected action in the future. As women's health expert Christiane Northrop puts it, "our body is the best health system we have - if we know how to listen to it." You may think you know your body, but you may have also gotten comfortable with what you imagine are its limits. This extraordinary piece of engineering is capable of much more than you may think.

Like our mind, the body craves stimulation and growth. Try breaking your usual pattern of movement and test your body's limits. Listen to what it is calling for. If you have spent a lifetime as an "unsporty person" it simply means you have not discovered the movement your body is looking for. You cannot have useful resilience until your body is working with all its potential power and ability. Now is the time.

Neurologist and author Oliver Sacks speaks and writes about the vast potential of movement and its effect on the brain. He notes, "much more of the brain is devoted to movement than to language. Language is only a little thing sitting on top of this huge ocean of movement." Exercise increases heart rate, which sends more oxygen to the brain. It releases chemicals and hormones that are related to cell growth in the hippocampus and other regions of the brain. We are only beginning to understand how different types of physical movement and different levels of exercise stress directly promote cell growth, memory retention and general brain health.

How you sleep

Sleep is an important part of Physical resilience, particularly deep Delta "slow wave" non REM sleep when your brain consolidates memories and washes out neural detritus. Deep sleep balances hormones and plays a role in regenerating cells in your body. In short, deep sleep is essential to your optimum Emotional and Physical function. Deep sleep is improved with vigorous exercise and a healthy diet.

Ideally you sleep 7-8 hours. If sleep is an issue for you, remove all electronics for the last 30 minutes before bedtime. Try a weighted blanket, silk pillowcase and/ or ambient "sleep noise" soundtrack (but make sure you are not seeing any blue light from the device playing the sounds). Good sleep habits have a host of flow-on benefits. Essentially, good deep sleep means you wake with the energy and stamina to be more productive and more engaged.

Remember, physical resilience is not about being the fittest body in the village. Physical resilience is about knowing your own body well, testing its limits, and keeping it strong and healthy. When Alice Walker observed that "the most common way people give up their power is by thinking they don't have

> *"To keep the body in good health is a duty, otherwise we shall not be able to keep our mind strong and clear"*
>
> - Buddha

any" she wasn't talking about physical strength or resilience - but she could have been. Don't sell your body short. Especially as you get older, especially if you are female, or you have health issues that make movement hard. Nurture your body, discover what it can do and empower yourself.

Thriving: Intellectual Resilience

Intellectual Resilience is the confidence in your on-the-fly thinking skills achieved by the practice of proactively seeking, digesting and applying new information without relying on prior expertise. Above all, Intellectual Resilience is about fostering curiosity. Curiosity enables us to problem-solve in an environment where our expertise is irrelevant or obsolete. Curiosity is vital to thriving in uncertainty both for its creative thinking potential and for the creative confidence it inspires. Being able to proactively wrangle your way through change - the key to EPIC Resilience - requires curiosity and confident creative thinking.

Stanford Professor Carol Dweck coined the term "growth mindset" in her book, *Mindset: The New Psychology of Success.* A growth mindset means you are constantly learning from new endeavors and failures, constantly embracing challenges and supporting others to do the same. Professor Dweck writes, "The passion for stretching yourself and sticking to it, even (or especially) when it's not going well, is the hallmark of the growth mindset. This is the mindset that allows people to thrive during some of the most challenging times in their lives." The opposite of the growth mindset is a fixed mindset that sticks safely to what the brain has already learned.

Most of us depend on a level of expertise to earn a living. Our thinking habits create the neural pathways we use to solve problems in the same way over and over and those neural pathways map our expert mind. We default to these pathways because they usually work for us. In our comfortable expert state we can become very focused and specialized. This can dull our curiosity towards areas that are not directly related to our expertise.

Developing intellectual resilience means actively working to maintain a growth mindset and not lapse into a fixed thinking state. As Zappo's founder Tony Hsieh observed, "it is never a question of not having enough resources, it's a question of not having enough resourcefulness."

In this era of exponential change we need to develop the habit of curious thinking as a strategy that runs parallel to our expertise. We need to develop our ability to consciously move between our expert thinking and our imagination. In addition, we need to develop the habit of questioning and listening, and to practice idea cross-pollination. These latter strategies are the way we constantly learn and they help us create the unexpected connections that form the basis of innovative thinking. The more widespread the information that you seek out and digest, the more accustomed your thinking will

"Do not be constrained by your present reality"

- Leonardo da Vinci

become to making unexpected connections and asking more complex questions, and the better you will become at leaping into the unknown with confidence. Creative confidence helps you identify opportunities in chaos while others are thrown into disarray by uncertainty and change.

Dealing with unpredictable environments or constantly evolving conditions outside our area of expertise involves operating in a state of mental bearable discomfort called Adventurous Thinking. Adventurous Thinking is an innovation strategy I developed, based on Howard Gardner's Theory of Multiple Intelligences and inspired by Edward de Bono's Six Thinking Hats thinking role play strategy. Adventurous Thinking uses five Lenses to provoke thinking out of expertise and into imagination and possibility. You can train yourself in this Adventurous Thinking mindset to provoke and practice mentally bearable discomfort and maximize your thinking options.

Strengthening Intellectual Resilience means honing your thinking to continually assess new information with a confidence not based in previous knowledge or experience. If your Intellectual Quadrant is weak, consider three aspects of your thinking habits:

> *"A pile of rocks ceases to be a rock when somebody contemplates it with the idea of a cathedral in mind"*
>
> - Antoine De St-Exupery

- How much new random information do you discover in a typical week? Random here doesn't mean social media stories or work-related material but fun facts, unexpected technical innovations, a different genre of music, basically morsels of information that are tangential to your usual preferences and day job.

- Are you a curious person? Do you generally ask many questions? Not socially interested polite conversation questions but questions about what you are learning, how somebody is doing something, what else an issue or item might contain or mean.

- Do you have people with whom you share and discuss ideas and concepts? This could be within a work context but it is the concept of openly sharing thoughts and ideas, listening to other people's thoughts and ideas, and giving constructive criticism or otherwise adding value to those ideas.

If you have answered "no" to any of these, fear not. These are all areas we can work on to strengthen your curiosity and help your Intellectual Quadrant flourish.

"Without a good question, a good answer has nowhere to go"

- Clayton Christensen

Intellectual resilience is essentially achieved by exposing yourself to information outside your areas of interest and forcing yourself to be curious. Asking questions will develop a habit of seeking out new knowledge. Below are some techniques to build this habit and reinforce your Intellectual Resilience.

A. Random Reading This is a simple way to improve your Intellectual resilience by pushing through the curated algorithms of the internet to expand your footprint for information collection. When you read a newspaper online your search engine and possibly the news source curates and personalizes the information you see. Every digital algorithm is about individual customization which means giving you information similar to that you have already read or searched for, in similar regions, in similar languages. The sameness of this information is the antithesis of Intellectual Resilience. In order to strengthen your intellectual resilience you need to proactively seek out unexpected information. When you browse a paper newspaper, rather than reading it online, various articles unrelated to your areas of interest will catch your eye. Make it a habit to read them. Browse random magazines when you can. Subscribe to Research & Development newsletters. Interesting informational tidbits are everywhere! Force yourself to seek out unexpected information.

B. Dig Deeper The digitization of reading material has fundamentally changed the way we digest what we read. Research from San Jose University describes a "new norm" in reading a screen called skimming, where the reader uses an F or Z pattern to word-spot through the text rather than digesting full sentences. Deep reading is the traditional way of reading every word, ideally grasping the complexity of the language, and creating thoughts around the concepts presented. Be conscious of your reading patterns. Be aware of when you speed-read or skim and make either mode an active choice instead of a default. Spend at least a few minutes every day deep reading new material and taking the time to think about its meaning. Sites like brainpickings.org present short thought-provoking written and visual pieces, making this exercise easy.

C. Fight the power   Try your Google search in another language or another region, and go to page 6 or further. Compare those results to your typical Page One Google search. I find interesting design inspiration when I use Google Translate to convert my search to French or Danish, then search as an image (because I can't yet read either of those languages). Intellectual resilience is about being aware of the level of curation we are limited by every day, and actively seeking to subvert that state and widen your exposure to new information. Again, it is about embracing bearable discomfort and understanding that the quick and easy search is not the only answer.

The Habit of Questioning

Questioning is a thinking process where we mentally dance around something that we don't know or understand, poking and

> *"Millions saw the apple fall, but Newton asked why"*
>
> - Bernard Baruch

prodding while we organize our thoughts to make better sense of it. Questioning works hand in hand with intently listening, and both are fundamental abilities for a growth mindset. In his book, A More Beautiful Question, Warren Berger talks about the progression of innovation-generating questions, starting with "Why?" then moving to "What if?" And finally "How might we?." If you are not in the habit of asking questions to learn new information or to inspire yourself, try this short exercise every day until it sticks.

Consider a piece of information you've just learned or a behavior you find odd. Ask yourself "Why is this so?." Then, "What if it were not?", and finally "How might I find another way?." This exercise is not about solutions. You are simply building the habit of provoking new thoughts by asking questions.

"I'm Curious…" Allow ten minutes to really put some thinking into this activity. Search "new technology" online and go to page 4 or further back. Alternatively, open a dictionary to a random page. Select an article or word at random and read and digest that new information for a minute or two. Now ask yourself "why might that be somehow relevant to the work I do every day?" Think

"We keep moving forward, opening new doors and doing new things because we're curious, and curiosity keeps leading us down new paths"

- Walt Disney

about that question and the other questions it raises. It is unlikely there will be an obvious link. Push yourself to think harder. Provoke your thinking with questions. What part of this new piece of information might be interesting to other people you know? Why might it NOT be interesting to the people you know? When we do learn something new we usually file that information for later without pausing to think, savor and swirl the new information around a little in our minds. We need to provoke the curiosity we were born with back into the forefront of our thinking and develop the habit of seeking out new random information. Exercise your brain by pausing and questioning around that new tidbit before it is filed away.

Deep Listening

In a group conversation, meeting or brainstorm, most of us are listening with the intent to find a gap and express our idea or opinion. Modern society generally works in a time-crunch where every part of our day is optimized to be productive and produce speedy results. That means the pressure is on us during meetings or brainstorming sessions to get as much done in as short a time as possible. This is not a good setup for the practice of genuine listening, and it means that many people are not properly heard or represented in the conversation that ensues. Learning to listen completely to another person and allowing that opinion or information to wash over your unfettered brain is a completely different experience. This deep listening is a very useful skill. As Stephen Spielberg observes, "When you listen you learn. You absorb like a sponge and your life becomes so much better than when you are just trying to be listened to all the time." Why is listening an important part of resilience? Because surviving and thriving in change means having the ability to learn and reason on the fly as well as being able to authentically connect with all kinds of people. Both these abilities are made more effective with genuine listening, listening with the intent to learn. Listen Up. Silence can be a more powerful tool than words. If you tend to be the speaker in a group and often find yourself carrying conversation or leading a discussion, it is time to discover the power of silence. I learned this many years ago as a young architect working for a wise businessman. In his office, discussing the building work on his house, he would ask his question and then pause and wait. In the early days I would rush to fill the silence and inevitably promise all kinds of extra work. Over time I recognized his strategy and I changed my response. I would answer concisely, then stop talking and just smile. We would sit looking at each other in silence. Instead of being disconcerted by the silence I became comfortable with it. This is a good communication skill to hone.

"When people talk, listen completely. Most people never listen"

- Ernest Hemingway

Thriving: Creative Resilience

Creative thinking is about proactively manipulating something using your imagination. Creativity doesn't have to manifest in a physical artifact. It is simply your act of translating a thought, an object or an environment through your personal lens. In terms of resilience, creative thinking is the ability to look at your environment and imagine the possibilities therein. Innovation is about making unexpected connections, and creative thinking is the means to that end. Confident creative thinking teamed with the curiosity you are developing in your Intellectual Quadrant sets you up as a consistently innovative thinker. This confidence in your own ability to imaginatively problem solve is as important to your resilience as the solutions you may come up with. When it comes to the potential of human thinking Einstein often says it best and here is a case in point: "Imagination is more important than knowledge. For knowledge is limited, whereas imagination embraces the entire world, stimulating progress, giving birth to evolution." In essence knowledge is the past and perhaps the present, and imagination is the potential of the future. In an era where social, political and business norms are actively disrupting and reforming, the ability to constantly imagine new alternatives and see possible connections between unexpected areas is extremely valuable.

"Creativity involves breaking out of established patterns in order to look at things in a different way"

- Edward de Bono

Many people associate creativity with artistic ability, and this can cause someone who "can't draw" to believe they are intrinsically uncreative. Not true! In fact research suggests that if a person who believes they are uncreative is given tools that provoke creative thinking and shown how to use them, they will deliver more creative output than people who think of themselves as creative but have no tools to prompt consistently creative thinking. SO - knowing that you are inherently creative and knowing that you can be taught to realize that ability and strengthen the habit of creative thinking, let us begin!

Believe The first step is simple: acknowledge to yourself that you are an intrinsically creative person with powerful thinking abilities. Stop whatever you are doing, stop your mind racing, and just be in the moment, letting thoughts wash over you. Your mind is vast and capable of incredible mental feats. Give it permission to wander without urging it to do anything specific. Just feel how it whips and wheels.

Unexpected Connections Creative thinking is beaten out of us somewhere during our education journey. British education innovator Ken Robinson describes how

> *"You can't use up creativity. The more you use, the more you have"*
>
> - Maya Angelou

western schooling was born of an industrial system that establishes silos of competency, regiments classes and hours, classroom layouts and teaching methods, and churns out specialists who are very capable at repeating what they have learned. This system ensures that any creative thinking is throughly expunged. To reintroduce our inherent creativity we need to work on a daily habit of forcing unexpected connections.

Our growth mindset embraces change and the energy and dynamism that this new thinking delivers.

"Creativity is just connecting things"

- Steve Jobs

Forcing creative thinking may sound counter-intuitive, but it is a curiously hard habit to set. This may be because, at school and in the workplace, creativity is usually seen as a "nice to have" stress reliever, rather than an essential ability that adds value. Remember how you are going to search random new information in "I'm Curious" as part of strengthening your Intellectual Quadrant? The simplest way to develop the habit of making unexpected connections is to extend that exercise another five minutes.

Forcing The Connection Habit Once you have given a new piece of information some thought, aggressively push yourself to make this new thing somehow relevant to part of what you do or what you think. For example: you may read about a new technology that is a very powerful fabric, inspired by the strength of a spider's web. Now spend an additional five minutes thinking hard about the possibilities of a such a technology in your life. If it can do that, what else could it do? Why would such strength be useful? How would you describe this new wonder to a child or to a much older person? If you see an image you love, or hear a catchy tune, give yourself five to consider what it is you love - color, beat, lyrics, topic - and how you might bring more of that to your day. Chances are you blank, but that is not the point. The point is that you flex your thinking muscle to push around what you know, and the practice taking jabs in the dark and possibly creating new connections between unrelated areas.

Re-Sharing Content Don't re-share content, co-create it. Our society is awash with content shared from one person to others without comment or critique. Many people share written content without even reading the entire piece themselves. Let us not add to the noise without moving the game forward. As Dumbledore observes to Harry Potter, "it is our choices...that show what we truly are, far more than our abilities." If you find something created by others to be powerful, moving or thought-provoking, by all means share it but add your own perspective to that creation when you share. Pausing to consider why this creation is powerful means you make a new connection between your spirit, values and purpose, and those of the maker. This connection is interesting and thought-provoking. Share that.

Sharing Ideas Never think that your idea isn't worth sharing. The most rewarding conversations can be with someone who listens and then builds up - or tears down! - a thought you have or an idea you are rolling around in your mind. So many people think ideas have commercial value and must be protected from others. Those of us who have non-stop ideas throughout the day understand that the idea itself is worth nothing unless you act upon it. Not every idea needs to be realized, but what better way to practice creation and make connections then to share ideas back and forth. A really exciting aspect of ideas sharing is that you will soon realize that the more ideas you share, the more ideas you have. As Quentin Tarantino observed, "the good ideas will survive." The rest are there to pique excitement, drive conversation and keep you mentally on your toes.

As a teenager I was fundamentally changed by this Socrates quote (often attributed to Eleanor Roosevelt): "Strong minds discuss ideas, average minds discuss events, weak minds discuss people." I have lived my live aspiring to discuss ideas, albeit with many lapses into events and people. Discussing ideas will maintain your happiness, increase your intellectual resilience and help you emotionally thrive.

III.
Resilience: Your Line in the Sand

THE AIM OF EPIC IS TO MAKE YOU AWARE OF THE STRENGTHS AND WEAKNESSES WITHIN YOUR QUADRANTS SO THAT YOU CAN AFFECT AND IMPROVE THEM. Self awareness is the key. Tony Robbins describes self awareness as "being aware of your own patterns," an ability he suggests is one of the rarest of human commodities. EPIC seeks to simplify your path to self-awareness by dividing those patterns into the four important Quadrants of self. Thus simplified, you can test your current levels of awareness in each of these Quadrants and then look at them as your whole self to assess where your relative strengths and weaknesses lie. The Line in the Sand is your starting point. We take the EPIC Quiz and then map your results on the Quadrant diagram to create your line in the sand.

The QR code below links to the online version of the EPIC Quiz and Quadrant diagram. You can choose to complete this Quiz online, or proceed using the following Quiz and Quadrant diagram in this book. The content is the same.

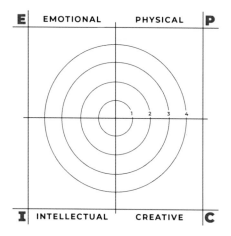

This is the Quadrant Diagram. It helps you create a visual of where your strengths and weaknesses lie and reminds you that our ideal is an evenly balanced whole. The numbered rings correspond to the answers in the Line in the Sand quiz. Once you complete the Quiz you can transfer your average results for each Quadrant onto this diagram.

The Line in the Sand is your first assessment. It allows you to explore your levels of resilience and self-awareness in each of the Quadrants using a simple EPIC Quiz. The result - your Line in the Sand - gives you a point of reference and something to work from. You can revisit this Quiz from time to time to check in on your progress in expanding your self awareness, strengthening your resilience and generally balancing these different aspects of yourself.

EPIC Resilience is about a growth mindset which means the work is never "done." Working to balance your Quadrants and strengthen the weaker areas allows you to survive: that is classic resilience. Once you have that solid foundation and balance, your EPIC work is all about thriving: strengthening your Emotional and Physical abilities and increasing your Intellectual and Creative confidence to face uncertainty and unexpected change with optimism and ability.

So now it is time to take the EPIC Quiz and determine your Line in the Sand. Please note your answers in each Quadrant and we will apply them to the Quadrant diagram at the end.

EMOTIONAL QUADRANT

Do you find it difficult to make decisions?
1. Yes, always
2. Often
3. Sometimes
4. Not at all

Do your relationships tend to have drama?
1. Yes, always
2. Often
3. Sometimes
4. Not at all

Do you consider yourself to have boundaries?
1. Not at all - what are boundaries?
2. Kind of
3. Yes, but I'm not great at enforcing them
4. Absolutely

Do you think about your values and how you apply them?

1. Never
2. Kind of
3. More often than not
4. Absolutely

Do your family, friends and coworkers understand what you will and will not tolerate in their behavior?

1. I've never really thought about it
2. Maybe, to some degree
3. I am working on making it clear
4. Absolutely

Do you feel guilty or anxious when you have to say no to people?

1. Yes, often
2. Sometimes
3. Very occasionally
4. Not at all

Do you ever feel disrespected by family or friends?

1. Yes, often
2. Not often, but yes
3. Sometimes
4. Not at all

Emotional Quadrant Tally: Are your answers mostly 1, 2, 3 or 4?

PHYSICAL QUADRANT

Do you consider yourself physically fit?
1. No
2. I am average
3. I am working on getting fitter
4. Yes

Do you know how physically strong you are?
1. I've never thought about it
2. I used to, but it's been a while
3. I have a fair idea of what I can and can't do
4. Yes, I know my strength abilities and limits

Do you wake up with energy?
1. Nope
2. Sometimes
3. Generally, yes
4. Absolutely

Do you get 6-7 hours of sleep most nights?
1. No, my sleep is terrible
2. Sometimes, but nothing is consistent
3. I'm working on getting more sleep
4. Generally, yes

Do you know roughly how many calories you consume in a day?
1. Nope
2. I have a fair idea
3. Generally, yes
4. Yes

Do you roughly keep track of how much protein you consume in a day?
1. No, I've never thought about it
2. I read contents but not specifically about protein
3. Generally I have a fair idea
4. Yes

Do you roughly know how many grams of sugar you eat in a day?
1. No, I've never thought about it
2. I read contents but not specifically about sugar
3. Generally, I have a fair idea
4. Yes

Do you actively access the nutritional value of food before you buy/ eat it?
1. No, I've never thought about it
2. I read contents sometimes
3. Generally, I have a fair idea
4. Absolutely

Physical Quadrant Tally. Are your answers are mostly 1, 2, 3 or 4?

INTELLECTUAL QUADRANT

How often do you seek out and digest new information not related to your work?
1. Never
2. Not often
3. Maybe once a week
4. Several times a week

Do you tend to read new information on a screen or in print?
1. Everything digitally/on a screen
2. Mostly screen, some print
3. Mostly print, some screen
4. I try to "deep read" with print as much as possible

What do you do with the new information you find interesting?
1. Look at it briefly and move on
2. Think about it
3. Share it with friends or colleagues
4. Actively try to apply it or discuss it with others

Do you consider yourself an actively curious person?
1. No
2. Somewhat
3. Yes, usually
4. Absolutely

Do you believe people are born with their intelligence? Or can it be improved?

1. You are born the way you are
2. IQ is basically genetic but maybe it can be tweaked
3. IQ can be improved with specific tools and techniques
4. IQ is a constant process of growth and can always be improved

Intellectual Quadrant Tally. Are your answers are mostly 1, 2, 3 or 4?

CREATIVE QUADRANT

Do you consider yourself a creative thinker?

1. No
2. Maybe/sometimes
3. I think so
4. Absolutely

Do you believe creative thinking can be learned?

1. Not really
2. Possibly
3. For most people, yes
4. Absolutely

Do you like to talk about ideas with others?

1. I've never thought about it
2. Yes. If someone else brings up an idea, I'll discuss it
3. Sometimes
4. Absolutely - it's my jam

Creative Quadrant Tally. Are your answers are mostly 1, 2, 3 or 4?

Now we apply these answers to the EPIC Quadrant Diagram to see holistically which of your areas are currently strong and which areas need work. If you are using the online version the Diagram will self-populate with your answers, and show you your Ring of Intent (more on that below). If you are working from the book here is an example of how to use the Quadrant Diagram.

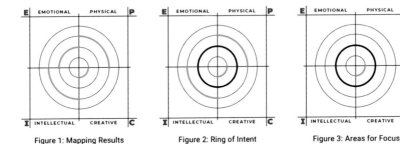

Figure 1: Mapping Results   Figure 2: Ring of Intent   Figure 3: Areas for Focus

In Figure 1 a person has taken the EPIC Quiz and noted their results for each Quadrant. In this case, they average 2 in Emotional, 3 in Physical, 1 in Creative and 3 in Intellectual. In order to create a visual of these results they have traced the lines of each circle corresponding with that number. The 1 circle is closest to the center of the diagram and 4 is furthest out. The aim is to expand as you strengthen, so the further out the better, but the aim is also to balance the Quadrants with a regular, connected circle.

Figure 2 shows the Ring of Intent, a balanced circle positioned equally between the highest and lowest number results. If you are using the online Quiz, your Circle will generate automatically. If you are using the book, you need to draw a circle midway between your outer and inner circle results.

Figure 3 shows how the Circle of Intent highlights the areas you need to focus on immediately. In this case, Emotional and Creative fall within the circle, which means that the Physical and Intellectual quadrants are good for now and this person should focus on the tools and exercises suggested in the Emotional and Creative parts of the book.

If this person takes the EPIC quiz again in 6 weeks, having worked on her Emotional and Creative Quadrants and maintained whatever she was currently doing in Physical and Intellectual, the results should all fall outside this existing Ring of Intent, meaning that person has improved her resilience and expanded her impact.

Now it's your turn to apply your results to the Quadrant diagram. Perhaps your average results mean that you have a perfect circle - Congratulations! You are balanced and can focus on generally strengthening every Quadrant and on connecting with more people. It is more likely though that you have two strong Quadrants and two lesser ones. Typically the Emotional Quadrant, with its complex content around values and boundaries, needs work. It certainly did for me!

Examine the Diagram and note which of your Quadrants are strong, scoring in the outer circles, and which ones need work. EPIC is about balancing, then expanding each Quadrant. First, growing with more thorough self awareness, then expanding with greater impact in your community and in the world. You are looking at your Line in the Sand: an overview of where you are currently at emotionally, physically, intellectually and creatively. You can see the areas that immediately need work - exciting stuff! This is your starting point for a new era of strength, resilience, growth and impact.

Set your Ring of Intent. This balanced circle, based on the median of your answers, will help you identify where to focus your immediate work. The Quadrants that fall inside your Ring can be improved using the examples and tools in this book. Those outside the Ring demonstrate your current strength and self-awareness. You can still work on those Quadrants, but focus on the weaker areas - those inside the Ring - first.

IV.
Balance Your Quadrants

"The most creative act you will ever undertake is the act of creating yourself"

- Deepak Chopra

SO NOW YOU HAVE COMPLETED YOUR QUIZ, SET YOUR RING OF INTENT AND YOU KNOW WHAT QUADRANTS YOU NEED TO PRIORITIZE AND IMPROVE. Please don't be daunted if it seems like a lot of work: just 5-15 minutes a day will quickly bring those lagging areas up to par. You will feel the difference.

Let me use my own Quadrant diagram to show how this process works. After a particularly difficult low point in my life I decided to spend a full day trying to define my issues and roadblocks and do some hard soul-searching and self-critique. I started with a classic SWOT (Strengths/Weaknesses/Opportunities/Threats) analysis of myself but quickly realized that a strong emotional and physical foundation paired with creative confidence would allow me to transform opportunities and threats proactively, on my terms. The division of my strengths and weaknesses into Quadrants made my situation easier to define and the work and balance easier to execute. I was eventually able to basically balance my Quadrants, rendering me more productive, way more healthy, more fun to be around and with renewed vibrant connections that help me lift.. The huge impact of that simple system of self-assessment and balance is what led me to write up this EPIC Resilience strategy.

Below is my original Quadrant check-in, mid 2019. Figure 1 shows that I was strong in parts of my Physical Quadrant - basically because I had thrown myself into fitness to try and cure my depression - and very strong in Intellectual growth, thanks to my work with other futurists at Singularity University. My Creative Quadrant was OK but some of my answers around connection and sharing were low (depression hits again). I was completely depleted in the Boundaries and Connection parts of my Emotional Quadrant.

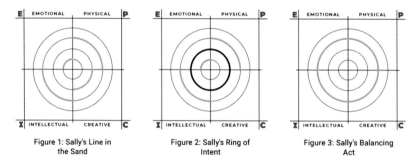

Figure 1: Sally's Line in the Sand

Figure 2: Sally's Ring of Intent

Figure 3: Sally's Balancing Act

Figure 2 shows my Circle of Intent. The off-balance of my Emotional Quadrant to my strongest Quadrants was so great that my Circle ended up right on my Creative result. This means that I needed to focus all of my attention on strengthening and growing my Emotional Quadrant until my responses brought results up to the edge of the Circle. I worked extremely hard to understand what was lacking in my Emotional Quadrant. I also worked on the Sleep aspect of my Physical Quadrant to give me more energy - emotional work is draining!

To sort through the Emotional deficit I sought professional therapy and expanded my reading (see the Further Reading chapter for a full summary of my research throughout this book). I finally realized the importance of Boundaries. I had never thought consciously about boundaries and it had taken just one unexpected and unorthodox life event to dramatically reveal this mid-life deficit. I worked hard to define and communicate my new-found Boundaries and my office walls remain covered in the quotes that inspired me to sort through my values and make some hard but rewarding decisions around them. I also proactively reconnected with people I had neglected while depressed and hunkering in place . These efforts lifted my Emotional Quadrant up to my Ring line and into balance with my other Quadrants.

Figure 3 is a recent result showing general balance and growth in all Quadrants. Once my Emotional areas balanced up to my Ring I looked at the diet aspects of Physical and the Connecting and Idea Sharing aspects of Creative in order to expand my Ring of Intent and generally become more resilient and proactive. Its that simple!

The growth mentality that comes with building these habits is energizing and exhilarating. That optimism is infectious and I have been able to share this system with others who see similar results. I continue to work on maintaining these new habits and I have redirected my main focus to outreach and connection. Now I am sharing EPIC with you.

V.
Level Up

SO MANY CULTURES DISPARAGE THE CONCEPT OF SELF-FOCUS AND BETTERMENT. Sometimes that is called Tall Poppy Syndrome, a cultural preference for "cutting down the poppy" that stands above the rest. The mistaken belief is that a person working on self-improvement must see themselves as better than those around them, and therefore needs to be "cut down to size" and humbled. Obviously Tall Poppy Syndrome cannot co-exist with a growth mindset. Luckily, having the strength to make time for self-care demonstrates you have the strength to withstand peer and work pressures. This strength is the essence of resilience.

Oprah Winfrey notes that "luck is preparation meeting opportunity." Chaos and change presents opportunity once EPIC Resilience has prepared you with a strong foundation from which to launch. EPIC resilience means you are flexible and primed - mentally and physically - to pounce.

Here we are, Quadrants balanced. You have Emotional, Physical, Intellectual and Creative stability and confidence. Is that it? Of course not! Renowned toughness expert David Goggins talks about how we use repetition to "callous our mind", making it less affected by feelings in the moment, and more able to toughen up and handle pain and adversity. Goggins talks about tackling head-on your weaknesses and the tasks you prefer to avoid head on, observing that the more discomfort you embrace, the stronger your mind becomes. When you become familiar with a level of bearable discomfort and begin to welcome that mindset as a source of dynamic energy you are truly ready to face change with confidence and aptitude. You are now ready to Level Up. It is the continuous learning of a growth mindset wrapped in 80's aerobic lingo because - I'm writing it! Leveling up means continuing to grow and improve to "next level" greatness. Leveling up your EPIC Resilience means not only checking regularly that your Quadrants are strong and balanced, but regularly practicing those EPIC habits, outlined under each Quadrant, to buttress and callus against mental and physical vulnerabilities. Leveling up is about regular self-maintenance so that you can now be of service to others. As Maya Angelou puts it, "do the best you can until you know better. Then when you know better, do better." There is no end, only self-awareness and betterment.

Your growth mindset means you will be constantly checking in with your Quadrants and confirming that complacency is not inviting pebbles into your shoes. Maintaining your EPIC self-awareness and skills means continuing to constantly share ideas, seek new experiences and find opportunities for personal growth. Your strengthened Quadrants make you Competent and they

> *"We are what we repeatedly do. Excellence, then, is not an act but a habit"*
>
> - Aristotle

make you Authentic. Our Level Up begins when we have a strong self-awareness and an internal strength founded on values, boundaries and mental and physical health. Your EPIC foundation means you are now in a position to effectively help others and strengthen that Connection aspect which makes humans feel truly fulfilled.

Your EPIC Resilience radiates an auspicious confidence which in turn inspires the people around you. Optimism is infectious and much needed around the world at any time. In times of tumultuous change it is more important than ever to transform people's widespread fear of uncertainty into hope. This is a most important aspect of resilience: the ability to lift and lead others out of fear and distress. Fear creates discord and disconnection. Where some people might be paralyzed in the face of new horizons and uncontrollable happenings, and others might be panicked that their expertise is no longer relevant, you have the confidence to think and react in a more agile manner and to share this ability with others.

That outreach and Connection element of Leveling Up your EPIC Resilience can take many forms. Here are a couple of suggestions: Head to your local coffee shop at a "before work" time and order your coffee to stay. Take a table or a bench, look around, and find someone to chat with. I've met some of my favorite people over coffee and my current Peet's coffee group has terrific discussions about ideas, politics and interesting perspectives with a flexible group ranging in age from 22 to 82. Never assume from first impressions that someone might not be interesting or interested in talking. At worst use the rejection to remind yourself that you operate as an EPIC individual without the need for external approval. At best listen, learn and share. Keep practicing those Random Reading & Unexpected Connections exercises at least once a day if you can. This habit makes you a font of interesting information brimming with ideas. Not only will you feel energized and full of potential, others will feel that energy also. EPIC confidence is optimism, and optimism is infectious.

Work proactively online by sharing informed ideas and opinions with people and groups you admire or aspire to. It is important that these concepts are your own: regurgitating other peoples writing or ideas is not the same. Don't hesitate to reach out and connect to people you respect. It is my experience that many of these people considered untouchable are in fact very interested in sharing original ideas and communications. Don't Neglect the Physical Quadrant. Staying in touch with your body through nutrition and movement is an essential part of EPIC resilience and effective thinking. Simply put, the mind/ gut connection is immensely important to your overall function and operating at peak potential means being aware of what your body needs. You don't have to be sporty to rock a strong Physical Quadrant, you simply need to nurture and empower your muscles with whatever form of movement works for you. Focus on your leg, shoulder and core muscles to keep your infrastructure strong. Minimize sugar and highly processed foods.

"Every time you are tempted to react in the same old way, ask if you want to be a prisoner of the past or a pioneer of the future."

- Deepak Chopra

It's that simple. Leveling Up means checking in with yourself each week, each Quadrant, and maintaining that level of self awareness and self care. Consider how these check-ins could help your family and friends. Consider what EPIC Resilience looks like for your workplace and your stakeholders. Resilience starts with each person being mentally and physically prepared, able, and confident, and then uses those people to propagate.

This book is not about motivating you for a day or two. EPIC Resilience is a way of life to help you to operate at your best, to be better and better, and to be better equipped to help others. Remind yourself, as often as you need to, that you are a pioneer of the future. There is no more important time than now to be resilient and level up. Go forth and be EPIC!

"There is always light if only we're brave enough to see it, if only we're brave enough to be it"

- Amanda Gorman

Notes, References, Definitions and Further Reading

Chapter 1: Finding Opportunity in Chaos

Buckminster Fuller   Buckminster Fuller was an American architect, prolific inventor and futurist who died in 1986. Best known for his work with geodesic domes, Fuller was an early promoter of biomimicry, or taking design inspiration from nature. His work around equality, inclusion and sustainability continues to remain edgy and relevant today. Fun fact: Fuller coined the term "Dymaxion", a fusion of the words dynamic, maximum, and tension, to sum up his mantra of "maximum gain of advantage from minimal energy input." Learn more about Bucky at the Buckminster Fuller Institute.

The Fourth Revolution   The World Economic Forum's 2016 report, *The Fourth Industrial Revolution: What it means and how to respond.* defines the concept of Fourth Revolution thus: "We stand on the brink of a technological revolution that will fundamentally alter the way we live, work, and relate to one another. In its scale, scope, and complexity, the transformation will be unlike anything humankind has experienced before.... The First Industrial Revolution used water and steam power to mechanize production. The Second used electric power to create mass production. The Third used electronics and information technology to automate production. Now a Fourth Industrial Revolution is building on the Third, the digital revolution that has been occurring since the middle of the last century. It is characterized by a fusion of technologies that is blurring the lines between the physical, digital, and biological spheres...."

The Singularity   Vernor Vinge coined the term in his 1993 article *Technological Singularity* and describes it thus: "The acceleration of technological progress has been the central feature of this century. We are on the edge of change comparable to the rise of human life on

Earth. The precise cause of this change is the imminent creation by technology of entities with greater-than-human intelligence. Science may achieve this breakthrough by several means:

- Computers that are "awake" and superhumanly intelligent may be developed.

- Large computer networks and their associated users may "wake up" as superhumanly intelligent entities.

- Computer/human interfaces may become so intimate that users may reasonably be considered superhumanly intelligent.

- Biological science may provide the means to improve natural human intellect.

Sebastian Junger Junger's documentary works, *Restrepo* and *Korengal,* sharing the life of frontline forces in Afghanistan, are gripping and insightful. His book, *War,* was similarly excellent and his short book, *Tribe: On Homecoming and Belonging,* 2016 is a must-read for insights into team-building and human motivation. You might know him as the writer of the book that made the movie, *The Perfect Storm.*

Professor Howard Gardner Gardner's books, *Frames of Mind* and *Multiple Intelligences,* were a huge influence on my Adventurous Thinking innovation mindset strategy and are used for education strategy across the world. Essentially Gardner proposes that the logical thinking forming the basis of most intelligence tests is only one of up to eleven intelligences that make up unique cognitive profiles for each person.

Stoicism Stoicism is a school of Hellenistic philosophy influenced by Socrates and the Cynics. Founded in Athens in the early 3rd century BC, Stoicism flourished in Greece and Rome until the 3rd century AD.

Emperor Marcus Aurelius wrote *Meditations* which is perhaps the most widely read Stoic text. Donald Robertson's 2019 book, *How to Think Like a Roman Emperor* is an accessible alternative.

Jane Goodall   Goodall's full quote is: "You cannot get through a single day without having an impact on the world around you. What you do makes a difference, and you have to decide what kind of difference you want to make."

Growth Mindset   Growth Mindset is a term coined by psychologist Carol Dweck in her 2006 book, *Mindset: the New Psychology of Success.* In a 2012 interview published on oneDublin.org Dweck says, "In a fixed mindset students believe their basic abilities, their intelligence, their talents, are just fixed traits. They have a certain amount and that's that, and then their goal becomes to look smart all the time and never look dumb. In a growth mindset students understand that their talents and abilities can be developed through effort, good teaching and persistence. They don't necessarily think everyone's the same or anyone can be Einstein, but they believe everyone can get smarter if they work at it."

Chapter 2: Understanding the Quadrants

Dr. Seuss   Seuss is one of my favorite creative thinkers. *Oh the Places You'll Go,* 1990 is the classic inspirational graduation present while *I had Trouble in Getting to Solla Sollew* is a terrific tale about self which I continue to periodically re-read. A fun fact on Dr Seuss: After the success of *Cat in the Hat,* his editor challenged him to write a book with only 50 different words. That book is his biggest seller, *Green Eggs and Ham.*

Annie Lamott   Lamott is a local NorCal writer whose book, *Bird by Bird* helped me get this book written. "No" is a complete sentence" is a great observation for everybody. I also particularly like "Lighthouses don't go running all over an island looking for boats to save; they just stand there shining."

Madonna   Madonna was a huge influence on my teen development.. Madonna demonstrated to this "weird" slightly outcast teenager that giving zero fucks about what other people think of you doesn't bring the world crashing down around your head: that in fact it makes you strong and it makes you - ironically - more interesting to others. She rocked heavy brows when all the moms were trying to pluck mine out. She rocked boobs and muscles when everyone aspired to be thin. She created a video with hot mermen. What an absolute legend! This quote is perfect: "I've been popular and unpopular, successful and unsuccessful, loved and loathed and I know how meaningless it all is. Therefore I feel free to take whatever risks I want." I too feel free to take whatever risks I want. Thank you Madonna!

Epictetus   Epictetus was a Greek Stoic philosopher, born a slave and influenced by Socrates and Hippocrates. Epictetus said many insightful, useful things and hugely influenced not only Marcus Aurelius and other subsequent power players but modern day thinkers like Albert Ellis, the psychologist who founded Cognitive Behavioral Therapy. Epictetus never wrote down his thoughts and observations: his endurance is thanks to word of mouth of his followers writing down his words. I chose this quote, "you should not have to look outside yourself for approval," to emphasize the importance of self awareness and confidence, but this one is also terrific because it highlights the importance of not allowing ailments or disabilities to hinder your thinking and your confidence: "Sickness is a hindrance to the body, but not to your ability to choose, unless that is your choice. Lameness is a hindrance to the leg, but not to your ability to choose. Say this to yourself with regard to everything that happens, then you will see such obstacles as hindrances to something else, but not to yourself."

Nipsey Hussle   Hussle was an American rapper and entrepreneur, also spelling his name Hu$$le, who was shot and killed in 2019. My daughter Jemima told me about him and his anti-gun activism and I came across that excellent quote, "If you look at the people in your circle and you don't get inspired, then you don't have a circle. You have a cage." Some people have told me this is a little harsh but I think it's fair. People don't have to inspire you 24/7 but if things are stagnant it's time to pull anchor, sail and progress. A letter from Obama read at his Memorial said, "While most folks look at the Crenshaw neighborhood where he grew up and see only gangs, bullets, and despair, Nipsey saw potential."

Rumi   Rumi was a 13th century Persian poet with beautiful thoughts. So many people I admire keep a book of Rumi close that I decided to do the same. "Life is a balance between holding on and letting go" speaks to the Nipsea Hustle quote too. Nothing is forever. Life is fluid. A sense of self will see you through it.

yung pueblo   Diego Perez writes as yung pueblo. I first saw his work on instagram and every post moved me and made me think. Check him out on insta @yung_pueblo

The NASA Innovation Lab   This lab, located in Mountain View, California, was the most exciting place to visit! I worked with some of the scientists and engineers to come up with more innovative grant proposals using my Adventurous Thinking strategy. In return they showed me urine that was turned into calcium in space, and told me about the annual Urine Cocktail competition they hold using these incredible filters that turn urine into drinking water. It was there that I heard about the quest for the best pump and the thought that ultimately Mars would be populated using a cyborg-type pump, some sort of perpetually living, machine-augmented thing. All their experiments with machines had been unable to significantly improve on the longevity and ability of the human heart.

John F. Kennedy JFK was renowned for his commitment to getting Americans of every age fit and healthy. He was ahead of his time in understanding the connection between physical health and mental and creative health.

Dr. Bessel van der Kolk van der Kolk is an American psychiatrist, researcher and writer specializing in post-traumatic stress and integrating therapy and science. His book, *The Body Keeps the Score* was a complete revelation to me and I have recommended it to scores of people. I believe this should be studied at high school level so that every person understands the direct connection between mental stress and physical stress, not only for themselves but for a better understanding of and empathy for the people around them.

Margaret Mead Mead was a somewhat maverick cultural anthropologist in the 1960s and 70s who applied her observations to American life. I particularly like this comment, "Children must be taught how to think, not what to think."

High sugar on the brain Here are a couple of studies on the relationship between high sugar and brain impairment:

J.E. Beilharz, J. Maniam, M.J. Morris, Short-term exposure to a diet high in fat and sugar, or liquid sugar, selectively impairs hippocampal-dependent memory, with differential impacts on inflammation, Behavioral Brain Research,Volume 306, 2016,ISSN 0166-4328, https://doi.org/10.1016/j.bbr.2016.03.018.

Giovana Jamar, Daniel Araki Ribeiro & Luciana Pellegrini Pisani (2020) High-fat or high-sugar diets as trigger inflammation in the microbiota-gut-brain axis, Critical Reviews in Food Science and Nutrition, DOI: 10.1080/10408398.2020.1747046

And here is a great article from the Harvard Health Blog first written by Eva Selhub, MD on November 16, 2015 and updated March 2020. *Nutritional psychiatry: your brain on food.*

Boxing   I used to abhor boxing: now I love it. That has to be a growth mindset in action! Initially I forced myself to learn about it because I was caring for someone who wanted to box professionally and the thought of the inevitable head injuries deeply disturbed me. I had to really push myself to be open, and I sought out a friend who boxed (big thanks to Colin!) to help me understand the appeal. Two years later I have a heavy bag and a speed bag at my house and I get great joy from boxing every two or three days. The feeling of strength is magnificent and I firmly believe all women should seriously try it and really discover the power of a good punch. I don't think I've ever felt aggressive when hitting the bag, I just feel empowered, fully present and essentially - well, fit as fuck! Boxing is an incredible workout and hands you a truly rock-solid core. I predict that if I ever make it into the ring for an amateur sparring match one hit on the head will cure me of my interest in fighting but for now it's a future adrenalin rush I look forward to. The technical aspects of the sport and the physical challenge intrigue me. Then again, maybe hitting the bag will remain enough…

Arnold Schwarzenegger Ah Arnie! I remember seeing The Terminator leaving Gold's Gym at Venice Beach on my first trip to the USA back in the late 80s. Such a presence! Most recently I thought his speech on riots and the attack on the Capitol really nailed what I was thinking, and this observation by Arnie will resonate with anyone who has almost been undone by a person or an event: "as shaken as we are by the events of recent days, we will come out stronger because we now understand what can be lost." Understanding what can be lost and taking on the challenge to never lose it is the path to being better.

Buddha I am most familiar with Thai Buddhism, the Theravada school, because in my early teens my family would spend summers in the north of Thailand. Buddha apparently visited Thailand around 250BC via India and Theravada or "School of the Elders" is the oldest existing Buddhist school. I find Thai and Cambodian Buddhas the most beautiful and powerful sculptures and Angkor Wat, with its multi-faced Buddha sculptures, is an incredibly spiritual place to sit and think.

Importance of explosive exercise on mental health There are many studies around this but the explanation that I've paraphrased below from the following study covers both the physiological benefits of increased blood flow to the brain and the flow-on mental health benefits as well.

Aerobic exercises have been proved to reduce anxiety and depression in two distinct ways. First, physiologically: exercise induces an increase in blood circulation to the brain, influencing the hypothalamic-pituitary-adrenal (HPA) axis which then communicates with several regions of the brain, including the limbic system, which controls motivation and mood; the amygdala, which generates fear in response to stress; and the hippocampus, which plays an important part in memory formation as well as in mood and motivation. Second: flow-on benefits from the physical action of exercising include distraction, self-efficacy, and social interaction.

Sharma A, Madaan V, Petty FD. Exercise for mental health. *Prim Care Companion J Clin Psychiatry*. 2006;8(2):106. doi:10.4088/pcc.v08n0208a

Christiane Northrop MD   Northrop is a pioneer in women's health and wellness. I particularly love her work around menopausal and post menopausal life. Like these observations:

"…menopause is an exciting developmental stage—one that, when participated in consciously, holds enormous promise for transforming and healing our bodies, minds, and spirits at the deepest levels…The woman in menopause, who is becoming the queen of herself, finds herself at a crossroads of life.…

from the new path another voice beckons, imploring her to explore aspects of herself that have been dormant during her years of caring for others and focusing on their needs. SHE'S PREPARING TO GIVE BIRTH TO HERSELF and as many women already know, the birth process cannot be halted without consequences."

I am currently reading her bestseller, the Oprah-endorsed tome, *The Wisdom of Menopause*. More people need to research and educate with this level of passion and optimism.

Neurologist Oliver Sacks   Sacks wrote many books observing the behavior of his psychiatric and neurological patients and his own brain. The movie *Awakenings* was based on his work.

The importance of sleep to mental and physical health   From the National Heart, Lung and Blood Institute website: "Studies show that a good night's sleep improves learning. Whether you're learning math, how to play the piano, how to perfect your golf swing, or how to drive a car, sleep helps enhance your learning and problem-solving skills. Sleep also helps you pay attention, make decisions, and be creative.

Studies also show that sleep deficiency alters activity in some parts of the brain. If you're sleep deficient, you may have trouble making decisions, solving problems, controlling your emotions and behavior, and coping with change. Sleep deficiency also has been linked to depression, suicide, and risk-taking behavior.

Sleep plays an important role in your physical health. For example, sleep is involved in healing and repair of your heart and blood vessels. Ongoing sleep deficiency is linked to an increased risk of heart disease, kidney disease, high blood pressure, diabetes, and stroke.

Sleep deficiency also increases the risk of obesity. For example, one study of teenagers showed that with each hour of sleep lost, the odds of becoming obese went up. Sleep deficiency increases the risk of obesity in other age groups as well.

Sleep helps maintain a healthy balance of the hormones that make you feel hungry (ghrelin) or full (leptin). When you don't get enough sleep, your level of ghrelin goes up and your level of leptin goes down. This makes you feel hungrier than when you're well-rested."

Leonardo da Vinci   Does anything further need to be said about this incredible thinker and original Renaissance man? An inventor of complex machines that were realized centuries later, a creator of painting techniques, a scientist and engineer. Da Vinci is a great example of holistic confidence and resilience supporting consistently adventurous thinking. At every Adventurous Thinking session I lead with this quote: "Do not be constrained by your present reality." Even as you consider your present it has passed. Looking forward requires you to push current knowledge to one side and dream with confidence.

Here is another da Vinci quote that pretty much sums up EPIC Resilience: "I love those who can smile in trouble, who can gather strength from distress, and grow brave by reflection. 'Tis the business of little minds to shrink, but they whose heart is firm, and whose conscience approves their conduct, will pursue their principles unto death." And of course this one, because action is growth: "I have been impressed with the urgency of doing. Knowing is not enough; we must apply. Being willing is not enough; we must do."

Tony Hseih of Zappos   Hsieh disrupted shoe sales by taking online a product based on fit and in-person service. Zappos pioneered the customer-first philosophy of friction-free returns and became the benchmark for online clothing sales and managing the expectations of online customers seeking fit. Hseih was the visionary who constructed the Zappos customer-forward strategy and the organizational structure of holacracy - a flat structure of self-organizing teams based on trust and transparency - at Zappos.

Exponential change   Linear progress is step by step: 30 linear steps = 30 years or meters depending on your measurement system. Exponential means constantly accelerating by constantly doubling, 30 exponential steps create an accelerating upwards hook as 1=2+4+8+16+32…continues to a total of over a billion yards or meters, or 26 loops around the earth. This scale is hard for the human brain to visualize, and the constant acceleration means that we have no horizon to set our goals to. Exponential change is a very different beast to linear improvement and requires different metrics and a different mindset to navigate with.

Adventurous Thinking   Adventurous Thinking is an innovation mindset strategy I started working on around 2008 and finally set as a strategy with Five Lenses in 2013 when I began teaching it at Stanford University. Adventurous Thinking is based on Gardner's Theory of Multiple Intelligences (see more under Professor Henry Gardner) and structured in a similar way to Edward de Bono's 6 Hats (see more below). Adventurous Thinking uses five diverse Lenses - Negative Space, Thinking Sideways, Thinking Backwards, ReThinking and Parkour - to throw the user outside their knowledge and expertise and into the thinking realm of possibility and imagination. I have taught it to Australian school teachers and their students as a system for injecting innovation into every subject, I teach it at Stanford and Singularity universities, to startups via Brazilian business educator StartSe and to various organizations around the world. EPIC Resilience is the foundation for consistently Adventurous Thinking, and Adventurous Thinking is essentially the growth part of EPIC. My EPIC workshops (www.adventurousthinking.com) include learning the Five Lenses as part of the Intellectual and Creative confidence aspects of EPIC resilience.

Maya Angelou   Angelou was an American poet, memoirist, and civil rights activist, working with Malcolm Luther King Jr and Malcolm X, who wrote the acclaimed memoir, *I Know Why the Caged Bird Sings*. Her insights are so inspiring; this one particularly resonates with me: "If you're always trying to be normal you will never know how amazing you can be," as does this excellent reminder about boundaries and self-worth: "Never make someone a priority when all you are to them is an option." The full quote, of which I've used a portion in my book, is, "You can't use up creativity, creative thinking builds on itself and increases the creativity of the thinker... You can't use up creativity. The more you use, the more you have."

Steve Jobs Jobs was a visionary, a dreamer who brought his imagination to life despite setbacks and failures, and impacted the entire world with his ground-breaking technologies. It was while reading some of Steve's thoughts that I realized innovation was, essentially, creating unexpected connections; casually or purposefully cross-pollinating in order to push people to their comfort limits and find new synergies. Here is Steve's full observation on creativity:

"Creativity is just connecting things. When you ask creative people how they did something, they feel a little guilty because they didn't really do it, they just saw something. It seemed obvious to them after a while. That's because they were able to connect experiences they've had and synthesize new things."

Edward de Bono de Bono is a renowned philosopher, doctor and inventor who coined the term "lateral thinking." I first learned about de Bono and his "6 Hats" thinking strategy, published in 1985, when studying architecture at Sydney University. Basically de Bono prompted a particular type of thinking when you "put on" a particular Hat and role-played that point of view, pushing through your implicit biases. The Six Hats are White Hat/facts, analytical, Red Hat/subjective, emotional, Black Hat/critical, skeptical, Yellow Hat/optimistic, Blue Hat/big picture, Green Hat/creative, out of the box thinking. I don't personally enjoy 6 Hat thinking but the strategy of using a device to provoke an atypical response is compelling and from this I devised my Five Lenses of Adventurous Thinking. As de Bono says, "Creativity involves breaking out of established patterns in order to look at things in a different way." He's right, regardless of whether it's Hats or Lenses.

Curiosity   Sir Ken Robinson is an education thought-leader who speaks and writes with great passion about the role of creativity and curiosity in education and his premise is simple: "Curiosity is the engine of achievement." Robinson has a terrific TED talk on creativity and education and is also very clear on the importance of practice and habit, observing that "You can't be a creative thinker if you're not stimulating your mind, just as you can't be an Olympic athlete if you don't train regularly."

Antoine de Saint-Exupéry   de Saint-Exupery was a French poet, pilot and adventurer who wrote and illustrated *The Little Prince*. One of the most successful world fairs of the 20th century, the 1967 International and Universal Exposition in Montreal, Canada, was based in part on this quote from de Saint-Exupery; "Être homme, c'est précisément être responsable. C'est sentir, en posant sa pierre, que l'on contribue à bâtir le monde" (*to be a man is to be responsible, to feel that by laying one's own stone, one contributes to building the world*).

Clayton Christianson   Christianson was an American business analyst and academic who developed the theory of "disruptive innovation." In his Harvard Business Review recap titled *What is Disruptive Innovation,* Christianson defines it basically thus; "Disruption describes a process whereby a smaller company with fewer resources is able to successfully challenge established incumbent businesses." Christianson's book, *How Will You Measure Your Life* had a great impact on me as it examines What to Think vs How to Think, and resource allocation in terms of your business vs family life. I first heard about his work listening to a talk by ex Caterpillar CEO Ed Rapp who had stepped down to fight his degenerative ALS. Despite his retirement Ed Rapp continues to inspire that huge company and its people with his values and transparency. Rapp talked about the influence of Christianson - so I bought the book.

Questions   *A More Beautiful Question* by Warren Berger is already on my suggested reading. A mind-boggling book chock-full of insights around the value and habit of questioning.

Skim and random reading   I first learned the term "skim reading" from an insightful 2018 article in *The Guardian* by MaryAnne Wolf titled *Skim Reading is the New Normal. The effect on society is profound.* Her subheading reads, "When the reading brain skims texts, we don't have time to grasp complexity, to understand another's feelings or to perceive beauty."

Cheating Google with Gabe Wyner   Back when I was a host on CreativeLIVE, an online education business, I was lucky enough to host Gabe Wynder and his series on learning languages. Gabe is an opera singer whose language learning system and app, FluentForever, changes the way we think about learning languages. My key takeaway, and one that I reference in the book and use often when working on bleeding edge research, is to google using image search, in another language, on another country's google, in order to find less curated information and to get a better understanding of nuance. The example Gabe used was the word "girl" in Russian. You might learn "girl" and assume you can refer to a new Russian friends' child using that term. However an image search of "girl" translated to "devushka" on Google Russia quickly demonstrates the word has a sexy element that is completely inappropriate for describing a female child. It is always an interesting exercise to see what nuances our cultural biases bring to words.

Walt Disney   I didn't get to the USA until I was 20 and the first thing we headed for after arriving in LA was Disneyland. What a vision! What an entrepreneur! Walt Disney literally brings dreams to life and his story of constant failure, of being told by employers that he was simply not creative, is enough to inspire anybody to learn from their setbacks and try again. In Disney's own words, "All our dreams can come true, if we have the courage to pursue them."

Neurological pathways and habits   Once we are around 25 years old our brain stops naturally forming new neural pathways and we become more "set in our ways". Neuroplasticity is about creating new neural pathways and discarding old ones, and the best way to stay neurally agile is to not get too comfortable in the way you think. The Adventurous Thinking strategy embraces this concept by pushing users into bearable discomfort. Imagination and probability thinking are part of this mindset. Neural pathways are neurons connected by dendrites, created according to our habits and behaviors. The pathway gets stronger with repetition - the way you solve problems for instance - creating expertise on the one hand, and a thinking rut on the other. The Growth Mindset and continued learning and idea-sharing are the keys to neuroplasticity. The habit you need to develop is that of remaining curious and constantly challenging your knowledge with new information and new possibilities.

Quentin Tarantino   Tarantino is a writer, actor and director who has created iconic films like *Pulp Fiction* and *Reservoir Dogs* that combine pop references, stylized violence and extremely quotable characters. A trademark is main characters with major vices rather than the classic Hollywood Hero" and I often use Tarantino to illustrate how my Parkour lens works because he likes to invert "normal" behaviors to shock and unsettle his audiences. As Morticia Adams once said "there is no normal. What is normal for the spider is chaos for the fly."

Deepak Chopra   Chopra is a celebrated holistic wellness and alternative medicine expert. I am a fan of his meditations with Oprah Winfrey; they are usually free, short and extremely refreshing. When I remember to do them! His clarity is inspiring.

Tony Robbins   Australians are traditionally opposed to the concept of "self help." That opposition goes hand in hand with the "Tall Poppy Complex" I reference in the book. This is an unofficial but cultural and widespread system to deal with those people we think are putting themselves "above us" - by thinking differently, by pushing new ideas or inventions - where those people are "chopped down to size" by social criticism, peer the derision and other collective habits. Tall Poppy is a large part of why I left Australia to pursue some of my ideas; I found the peer criticism and bitching about my inventions and general lack of support for invention disappointing. So being an Aussie in California I started hearing a lot from friends who had attended transformational Tony Robbins seminars, and being an Australian I was initially extremely skeptical about his "godlike" standing in the business and self help communities. Then I watched the documentary *I Am Not Your Guru* and understood the appeal of Robbins. Although I don't agree with some of the very masculine motivators I do appreciate much of the mind reset work Robbins has mastered. That documentary is well worth watching. One of Robbin's most EPIC observations is, "the only thing that's keeping you from getting what you want is the story you keep telling yourself."

RECOMMENDED READING

A More Beautiful Question by Warren Berger. Bloomsbury Publishing. 2014..

Animal Wise: The thoughts and emotions of our fellow creatures by Virginia Morell. Crown Publishing 2013

Frames of Mind: The Theory of Multiple Intelligences by Howard Gardner. Basic Books 1983.

Frugal Innovation: How to do more with less by Navi Radjou & Jaideep Prabhu. Public Affairs.2014.

How will you measure your life by Clayton Christianson. Harper Publishers.2012

The Four Agreements by Don Miguel Ruiz. Amber Allen Publishing.1997

The Influential Mind by Tali Sharot. Henry Holt& Co. 2017

The Geography of Thought: How Asians and Westerners think differently - and why. By Richard E Nesbitt. Free Press 2003.

The Toaster Project by Thomas Thwaites. Princeton Architectural Press. 2011

The wasp that brainwashed the caterpillar: Evolutions most unbelievable solutions to life's biggest problems by Matt Simon. Headline Publishing 2016

Thank you

HEARTFELT THANKS TO OLIVIA, JEMIMA AND SIMON FOR NOT ONLY ENCOURAGING THE CONCEPT BUT READING, SUGGESTING, EDITING AND BUOYING ME UP WHEN IT GOT A LITTLE OVERWHELMING. Olivia designed my cover as well - thanks Liv! And Jemima created the end graphic - thanks, Dotsy! To Jeanne who not only bank-rolled the Quadrant graphic and gave me endless encouragement but was also the brains behind the EPIC anagram (while I was pondering PICE and CIPE. lol) you always come through my friend and I love you. To Eduardo from Amazing Experiences, I so appreciate your limitless enthusiasm, input and energy for Adventurous Thinking and EPIC and I look forward to rolling out our corporate certification program with you! To my big-hearted and diligent reader friends Tanya, Shari, Cole, Sara Jane and Lysandra thank you for your time and your thoughtful comments. To my fabulous sister Poppy thank you for reminding me of the Aussie POV but even more - thank you for generously, miraculously fitting this in between a super career, three young kids, a stay at home order and a Masters. You are truly EPIC. To my Peet's crew who encourage me to realize every mad idea and often tender their own, and in particular Dean, Brad and Erin who tried the original EPIC daily video concept - thank you for indulging the crazy! Thanks Dan for keeping me on track. Thanks Colin for introducing me to boxing. Thanks to professional counselors Gary Fedoroff, an addiction specialist, and David Kest who helped me better understand myself and others. And finally thanks mum for the non-stop-creative brain and thanks dad for the gene of huge optimism that has seen me innovate, experiment, invent, fail and get up again over and over and over. Jono - thanks for your endless belief that I can do anything. Benno - "supercynic" - love your random check ins. It took a village. It still does. I bloody love my village. Thank you!

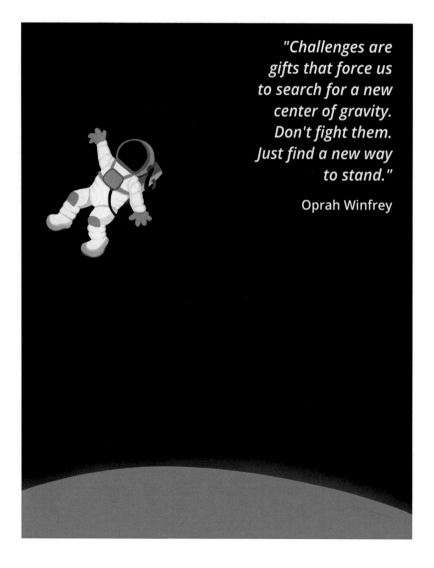

"Challenges are gifts that force us to search for a new center of gravity. Don't fight them. Just find a new way to stand."

Oprah Winfrey

About the Author

"The greater optimists dream of what could be. Not in a romantic sense. Much much bigger. That's where I try to exist for as much of my time as possible"

- Sally Dominguez

SALLY DOMINGUEZ IS A FUTURIST, AN ENTREPRENEUR AND A THOUGHT LEADER IN RESILIENCE AND INNOVATION. An Australian inventor and innovator Sally co-hosted *The Next Billion Cars* podcast and Foxtel's *Aussie Inventions that Changed the World,* judged inventions on ABC TV's *New Inventors* and judges Car of the Year awards. Sally's multi-award-winning products, Nest High chair and the Rainwater H2OG tank, are recognized globally: Nest is held in the Permanent Collection of the Powerhouse Museum and Rainwater HOG is in the Museum of New York and was named one of the USA's Top 10 Green Building Products. Sally's design work is featured in *Cool Green Hunting, Design Like You Give A Damn, Secrets of Top Designers* and NSW Design Technology textbooks. She is an Ambassador for Good Design Australia and in 2012 she was named one of Australia's "50 for the Future" innovators working in Silicon Valley.

Sally is on faculty at Singularity University as an exponential (10X) Mindset specialist and she was IKEA's sustainable resilience expert for their *2020 Life at Home* report. Current projects include working with IADB to spearhead green hydrogen innovations in the Caribbean and working with UK transport designers Quarterre to co-create a new house/vehicle hybrid for resilient nomadic communities. Sally teaches her Adventurous Thinking strategy, a proactive design thinking methodology, at Stanford and to organizations around the world. In 2018 she developed Adventurous Thinking into a pilot STEAM strategy, SYSTEMIC, for Australian school students.

Sally's skill is inspiring and assisting others to think consistently in the realm of possibility and curious thought. Her passion is spreading optimism and leveling up human potential as a response to this new Machine Age. Sally lives in Marin County, USA with Simon, Olivia, Jemima, two dogs, two rabbits and excellent neighbors. Fun fact: Sally and her car mate Sammy Stevens were the first Australians to drive the grueling 8-day off-road Rallye des Gazelles across Morocco

Go to www.sallydominguez.com or scan the barcode directly below to learn more about Sally's work and areas of expertise.

Made in United States
North Haven, CT
15 November 2022